Echoes Of Ataraxia

Whispers of calm.

~Azeera Naseer

To the voice that keeps whispering in me,

Thank you — because of you, this book exists.

Author's note

This is my debut poetry collection—the very first time I'm sharing my voice and heart in this way. Thank you for joining me on this incredible journey; your support means the world to me.

This poetry collection ultimately aims to help you find yourself a friend within you. A voice, that you would want to hear when life feels harsh. A voice you might be quite familiar with. Each poem, is unique in its own way and echoes the thoughts you might be scared to whisper.

This book is a reminder that being "enough" isn't about fitting inside a box but about embracing the full spectrum of ourselves—messy, beautiful, and evolving.

Thank you for touching this book, buying it and willing to embark on this journey with me.

May these poems remind you that you are never alone, and that your story—*just as it is*—is worthy of being heard and cherished.

With love and deepest gratitude,
Azeera Naseer

"A quiet fire, embraced by waves of peace"

I Don't Know Who I Am When No One's Watching?

There. I said it.
I don't know who I am when no one's watching.

To some, I'm kind.
To some, I'm stubborn.
To some, I'm a cry-baby.
To some, I'm bold.
To some, I'm mature.
To some, I'm childish.
To some, I'm trash.
But to some, I'm a masterpiece.

But what if no one's watching?
What if there are no eyes to criticize me?
No voices to echo who I'm supposed to be?

Who would I be—
to *me*?

Who would I be
if I wasn't trying to live up
to who I *think* I am?

Who would I be?

I'd say I come from a Broken Home

I don't think there's much difference
between a broken home and a perfectly decorated
house.

In that case, I'd say I come from a broken home.
Because no matter how shattered a home is,
it's still better than a house
with lights hanging and new furniture,
but nothing holding it together.

I'd say I come from a broken home—
and still be proud.

Because after all,
I come from a *home*, not just a house.

Isn't that a privilege?

Spectrum of Me

I don't know what my second favourite colour is.
Wait—
I'm not even sure about my favourite one.

Sometimes, it's black—
the comfort of shadows,
the way it holds everything and says nothing.

Sometimes, it's white—
a blank page,
a new start.

Strange, isn't it?
How my own perspective clashes.
How my own opinions contrast.

Maybe that's why I can't choose.

Because I am not one shade.
I am shifting tones,
a palette of contradictions
that still somehow blend.

And maybe that's the point—
that I don't have to settle on a single favourite colour
when I've been learning
to love the entire spectrum
that is *me*.

Hypothetically...

What if clocks ran backward—
unwinding the hours we thought we owned?
What if the time we're waiting for
is just a name we gave for longing?

What if mirrors lied?
What if the reflections we trust
are mere illusions and not truth?

What if fire gave us chills,
and we were the ones
who named the sting a burn?

What if rain fell upward,
and we just called it down?

What if we walk behind our shadows,
not ahead—
always trying to catch up to something
that was never chasing us?

What if?

Hypothetically…
what if?

The Moon

Though not whole all the time,
still receives immeasurable love.
And you think you are unworthy of love?

Think again

HONEY RAIN

What if, when it rains, you arrive—
and the storm forgets its sorrow,
sweetens its tears,
and suddenly,
the *sky cries honey?*

You may love tea.

But don't convince yourself you love coffee
just to fit in.

(Maybe the same goes the other way too.)

White pencils

You will surely feel useless
until you discover your own worth.
Like a white pencil
amongst a set of vibrant colour pencils.

All you need to know is this:
you weren't made for the standard, usual white
paper
You need a black sheet,
a different origin.

But until you realize this yourself,
you'll feel useless.

Remember —
you are *not*.

In One Way or Another

To be loved is to have a mom who asks if we're full,
even after the extra dosa she served.
To be loved is to have a dad who tears up when you
fall—
but is pretty good at pretending he didn't.
To be loved is to have the privilege of fighting with
your siblings.
To be loved is to have yourself to hold you when no
one else does.
And in that case, aren't we all loved?
In one way or another, aren't we all loved?

KINTSUGI

Kintsugi—an artform that life offers us.

An art we're never taught, but somehow learn.
It teaches us not to hide our flaws,
but to embrace them—boldly yet gently.

After all, aren't our scars the proof
that we *tried*,
that we *broke*,
but still chose to rebuild?

And when we mark them with gold,
we're not just mending—
we're honouring the effort it took to heal.

I Love the Ocean

"I love the ocean!"
"Well, prove it," they said.

So I thought—
standing on the shore,
waiting for a wave to dash against my feet,
would prove my love.

But rethinking it,
I realized it would be selfish
to drain my remains
into something I love.

So I thought swimming would prove my love better.
Yet what is love,
if it is moving my hands and legs back and forth
with all my force?

Is it love
if my gentle hands
cut through the water I say I love?

And so, I stand there—
on the brim of the shore—
waiting for a wave to pull me in.

As it did, I slowly immersed myself in the ocean.
My legs froze; hands motionless.

Yet I breathe.
Once, I think.
Air bubbling through my nostrils and mouth.

And there—me, drowning into the sea:
a perfect sight of love.
Of how I would hurt myself
to not hurt the water.

And there—me, sinking deeper:
a perfect sight of love.

Maybe now they're convinced
that I love the ocean.
That I love the ocean more than myself.

But this **isn't love**.
Love doesn't hurt.
Maybe it does—
but not this much.

Yet this once,
I'll awfully convince myself otherwise...

Autumn

A season between summer and winter.
An emotion between chaos and calm.

If I were to be a season,
I'd be autumn—
a symbol of change,
a sign of acceptance.

Of how, to bear new leaves,
old ones fall.

Strangely Beautiful

It's strangely beautiful how everything around us
has a sense of feeling,
An emotion within.

That when the cloud feels heavy, it pours.
The cry, the rain; Though an effect of something
painful,
still seems beautiful.

And it's strangely beautiful how, when it rains,
it washes away even the heaviness inside our chest.
Strange, isn't it?
But strangely beautiful, I'd say.

That sometimes, it's okay to cry.
It's okay to cry and pour out everything that hurt.
But once you're done, remember:
what's gone is gone,
and what's best for you is yet to come.

Sometimes, I'm like fire—
burning and biting with harsh truth,
constantly trying,
radiating light that somehow stings.

Sometimes, I'm like water—
mediating the mess in me,
trying to wash away
everything that hurt.

I am both fire and water, The fury and the
forgiveness
all at once.
And somehow,
that's my *greatest* strength—
and my terrible *weakness*.

Wish I Knew

Dear love,

Oh! I wish I knew I'd write to you,
About the way your tides cleanse my feet.
How, when they do, they don't just cleanse my feet;
they cleanse my soul.

Oh! I wish I knew I'd write to you,
About the secrets you murmur to the shore,
How the shells embrace your whispers,
As memories too dear to hold.

Oh! I wish I knew I'd write to you,
About the ache in my voice and the pain in my words,
And yet, how I write to you despite all of it.

Oh! I wish I knew I'd write to you,
I wish I knew a bit earlier,
How, every time I look at you,
You heal something, I never knew was broken in me.

An Empty Chair

It's clean. Polished. And empty.
Waiting for something, someone.
And here I am, wishing upon every star,
that the chair gets occupied
and I finally receive the love I need.
And here I am, gatekeeping the chair—
not letting even a speck of dust land on it,
because who will sit on a dusty chair?
Who will ever want to?
And if no one does, how will I receive love?
How will I fill my voids and mend my cracks?
It all felt like a mess. Until I realized,
I could've sat in the chair.

I COULD'VE SAT IN THE CHAIR.

To the weary

Don't cry for the people you lose—
the ones lost to time,
and the ones lost to love.

The ones you believed were forever,
and the ones you believed you were good for.

Don't cry, dear wandering souls,
for I see your plight—
the way you whisper heartbreaks
into my vast, listening ear.

I see you.

So, dear weary people,
let not another teardrop
know what your cheek feels like,

For I see you, I know you. And you're never alone.

~ Night Sky

A Letter from the Universe

Oh darling, don't be so harsh on yourself.
For you are a reflection of me, and that somehow
makes me proud.

Don't believe them when they say you're full of flaws.
For you are a reflection of the infinite light I possess.

Don't believe them when they say you're a mess.
For you are a reflection of the trillion stars—shattered
yet still shining.

Don't believe them when they say you're ugly.
For you are a reflection of the galaxies I hold.

Oh, dear darling, remember:
You are an ethereal mixture of stardust and cosmos.
Remember, you hold potential—far more than you
think.

You weren't made just to survive.
You were born to live.
To live the life you're yet to discover.

Remember, you are the universe in motion.
And I've been waiting for you to realise your power.

~ *The Universe*

I'm too much and never enough.

I'm like the sun —   I
have the light you look up to,
but I'll burn you if you come a little too near.

I'm like the sea —
I hold enough water to quench your thirst,
but who wants to drink salt water?

I'm like the rain —
I pour myself over you to revive your soul,
but every household has an umbrella.

I am both too much and never enough.
And maybe… that's why I'm like this.

The fourth dimension (*TIME*)

If time could apologize,
would it be sorry for taking you away from me?
Or would it say it should've never let us meet at all?

If time could apologize,
would it pity mothers who look up to children who
left them,
or would it blame itself for treating those children
harshly?

If time could apologize,
would it cry at graveyards,
or would it calm the hearts shattered by the loss of
those they once loved?

If time could apologize,
would it go back to the days when war shattered
more hearts than land,
or would it rather apologize for the wars we fight
with ourselves every day?

If time could apologize,
would it take the blame—
or would it blame us?

You are
allowed
to pause.

Things we forget

One, wake up before the alarm.
Two, brush your teeth, cleanse your body,
even before you've processed the day ahead.
Three, get into clothes that you don't really feel
comfortable in;
Clothes that don't really feel like *you*.
Four, eat a cup of bland food,
and pretend you're already full.
Five, leave the house before you're late.

Six, life isn't going to end if you don't get this order
right.

Get that inside your head.

Even Broken, Still Loved

Not everything that is broken needs fixing.
Maybe sometimes, keeping your favourite coffee
cup—cracked, chipped;
tucked away on the shelf,
not having the heart to throw it away,
is the purest form of love.

Maybe sometimes,
love is better explained not in the things we do,
but in the things we choose *not* to.

Fly

Sometimes, the reason we underestimate ourselves
is because no one ever saw our true potential—
not even us.

Even birds learn to fly when they fall—
not when they are given a land to walk on.

River

I know my final goal. Yes, I do.
To reach the vast ocean — that's what I'm made for.
Yet it takes me so long to get there —
to feel what the tides feel like,
to embrace every shell
and gently cleanse it.

But without the bends, without the breakage,
without the pause, the hurt,
I would never have reached eternity.

And so, dear souls —
just like me, you, too, must face hurdles.
Not to destroy you,
but to help you discover
your truest strength,
your deepest flow.

~ River

Would You Still Pick Roses?

Would you still pick roses
if they lost their colour?
If their thorns grew sharper,
and their fragrance faded?

Would you still pick them—
regardless of losing everything
that made them special?
Would you?

If you would,
then why wouldn't you do the same with humans—
the ones who are more beautiful
than any flower ever?

Thank You

Thank you so much for reading my poems and sharing this journey with me. Your support and kind words mean the world. I hope these words have touched your heart in some way. Please stay connected — there's so much more to come!

About the Author

Azeera Naseer is a 15-year-old poet who has been writing for nine years. This debut poetry book marks her first milestone in a lifelong journey of creativity and self-expression. Azeera draws inspiration from her love of tea, the ocean, and the moon—often weaving these elements into her poems as metaphors for life's deeper emotions. She believes poetry should be a space free from limitations, allowing readers and writers alike to express their truest selves, which is why she writes in free verse. Though just starting out, Azeera looks forward to growing as a poet and sharing more of her voice with the world. Your support means everything to her—please follow her on Instagram at @Azifcreations and share your thoughts and reviews. Thank you for joining her on this journey!

www.ingramcontent.com/pod-product-compliance
Lightning Source LLC
Chambersburg PA
CBHW020511160726
47991CB00007B/2906